HAPPY
BIRTHDAY
BROTHER!

This is your day!
BROTHER!
Start at the X to help your party guest reach the puppy. Then color the pictures.

X

Connect the dots and color your birthday party guest!

The sheep sends birthday
wishes to an awesome
BROTHER!

Start at the X to complete the maze. Then color your birthday balloons.

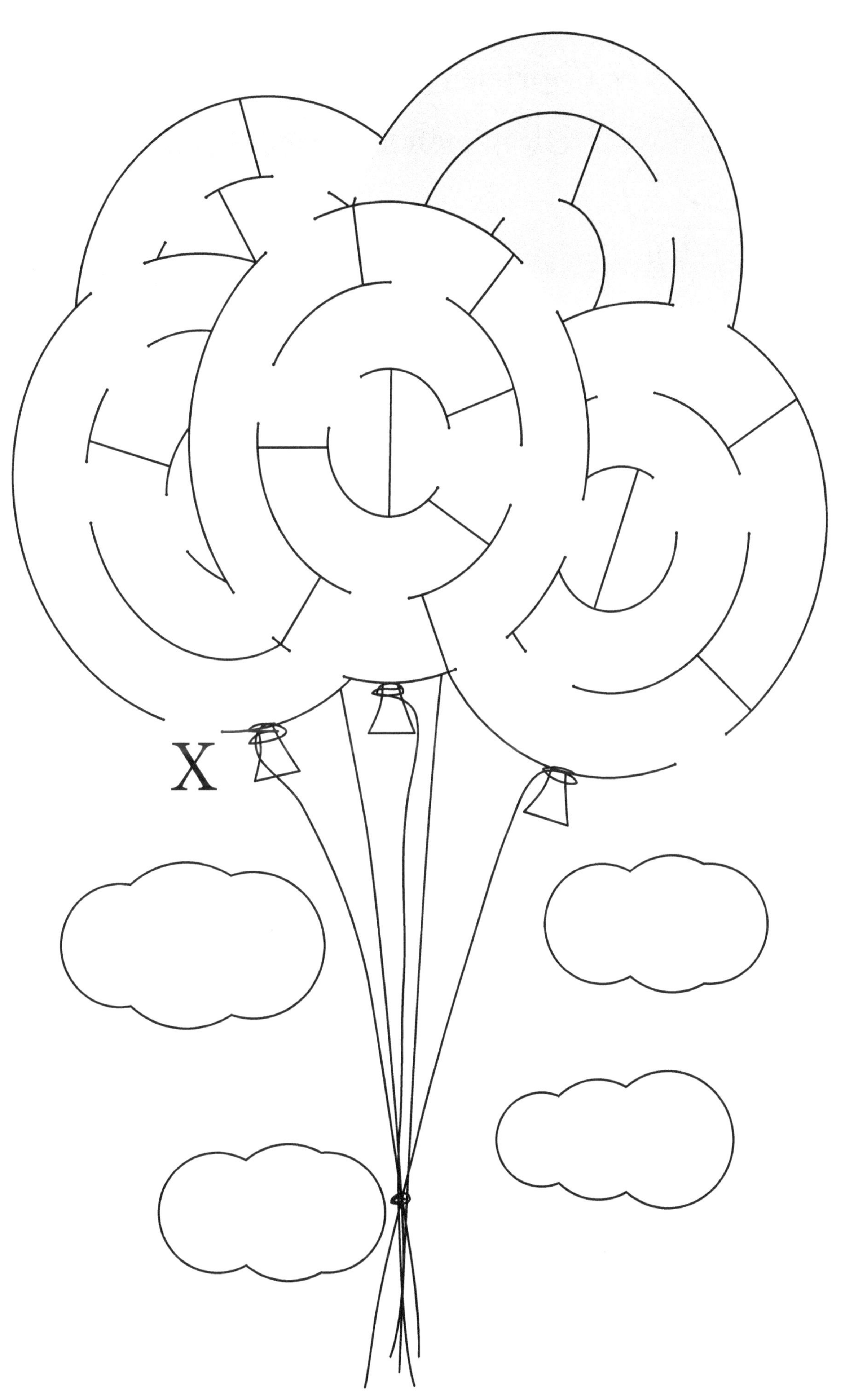

X

Connect the dots and
color your cupcake.

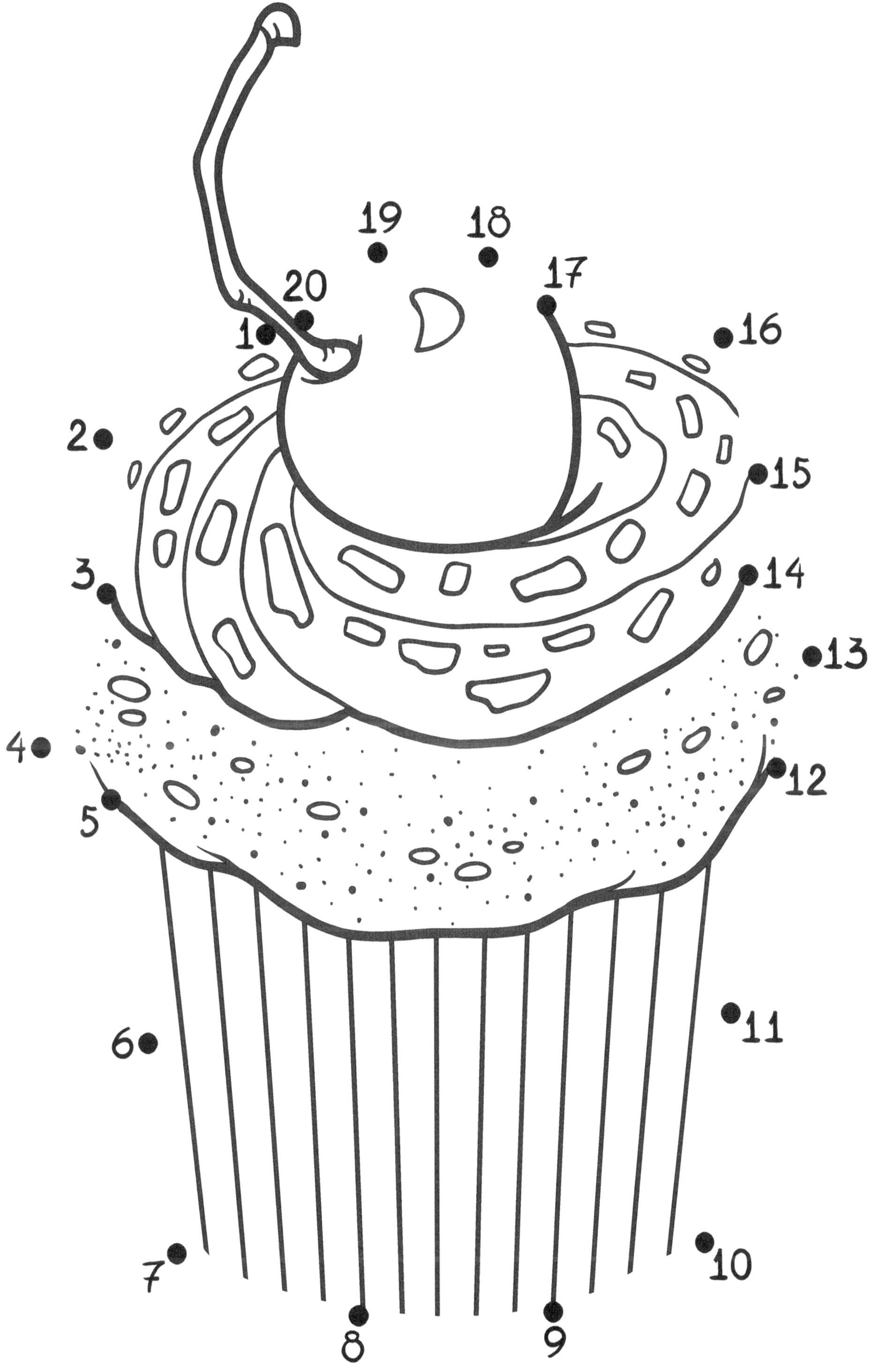

Count the number of candles, cherries, and strawberries on the cake.
Bonus: What's the total number of decorations on the cake?

_____

HOW MANY ?

Color, cut, and glue the cake on another sheet of paper. What is your favorite flavor?

CUT & GLUE
COLOR
CUT OUT
GLUE
USE EXAMPLE OR YOUR IMAGINATION
1
2
3

Color the party reindeer!
The reindeer wants to join
the celebration with an
amazing BROTHER!

HAPPY
BIRTHDAY

Start at the X to help the kitten reach the cupcake.

X

How many diamonds, hearts, and circles do you see on the cupcake?

Bonus: What is the total number of decorations? _ _ _ _ _

HOW
MANY ?

Start at the X to complete the maze. Then color your party hat!

X

Color the ice cream cone. Then cut and glue the cone on a blank sheet of paper.
What is your favorite flavor of ice cream? ________________

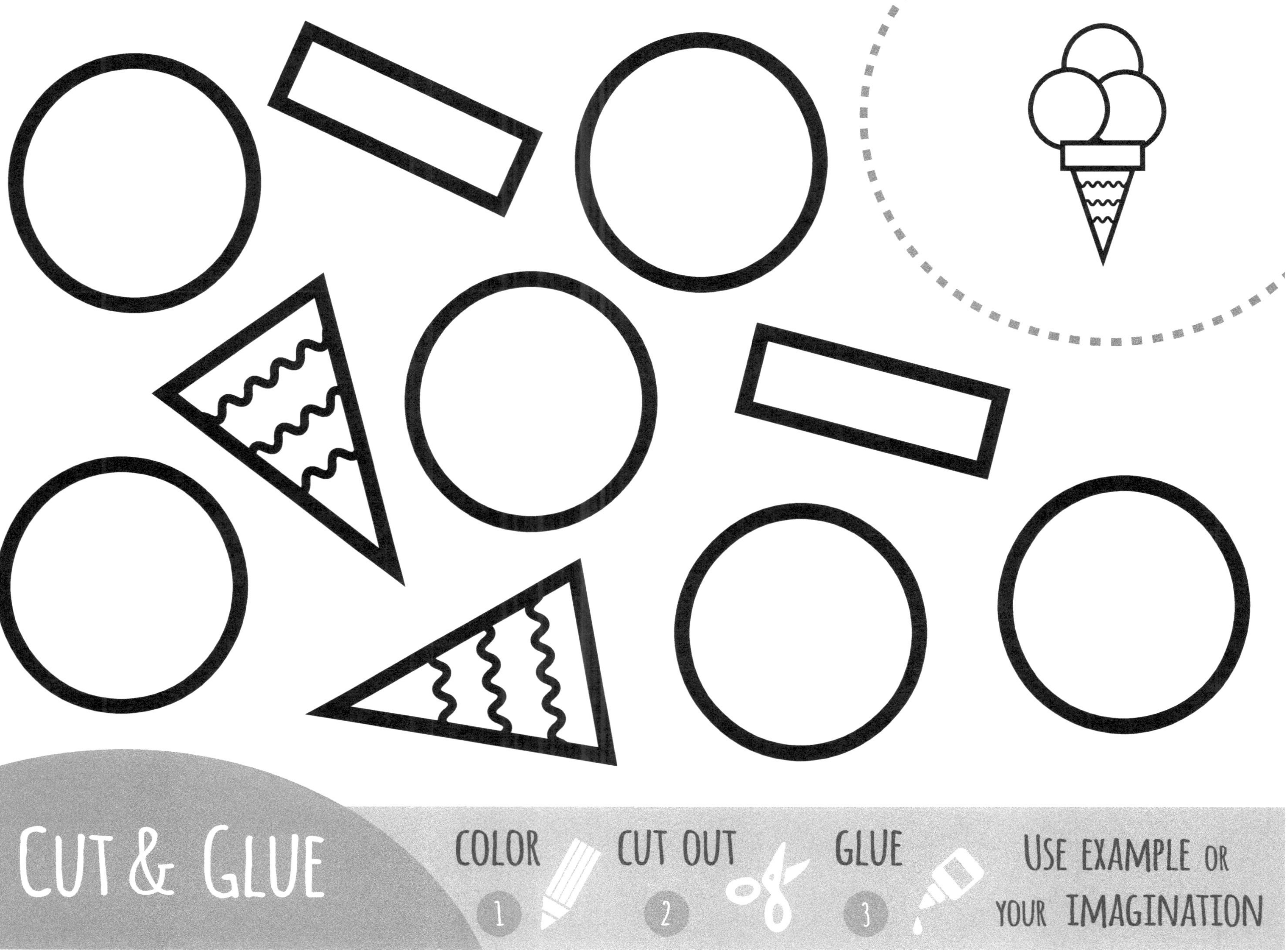

CUT & GLUE
COLOR
CUT OUT
GLUE
USE EXAMPLE OR YOUR IMAGINATION
1
2
3

Color the hippopotamus. The hippopotamus sends warm birthday wishes to a delightful BROTHER on this very special day!

HAPPY
BIRTHDAY

Connect the dots and
color your birthday present.

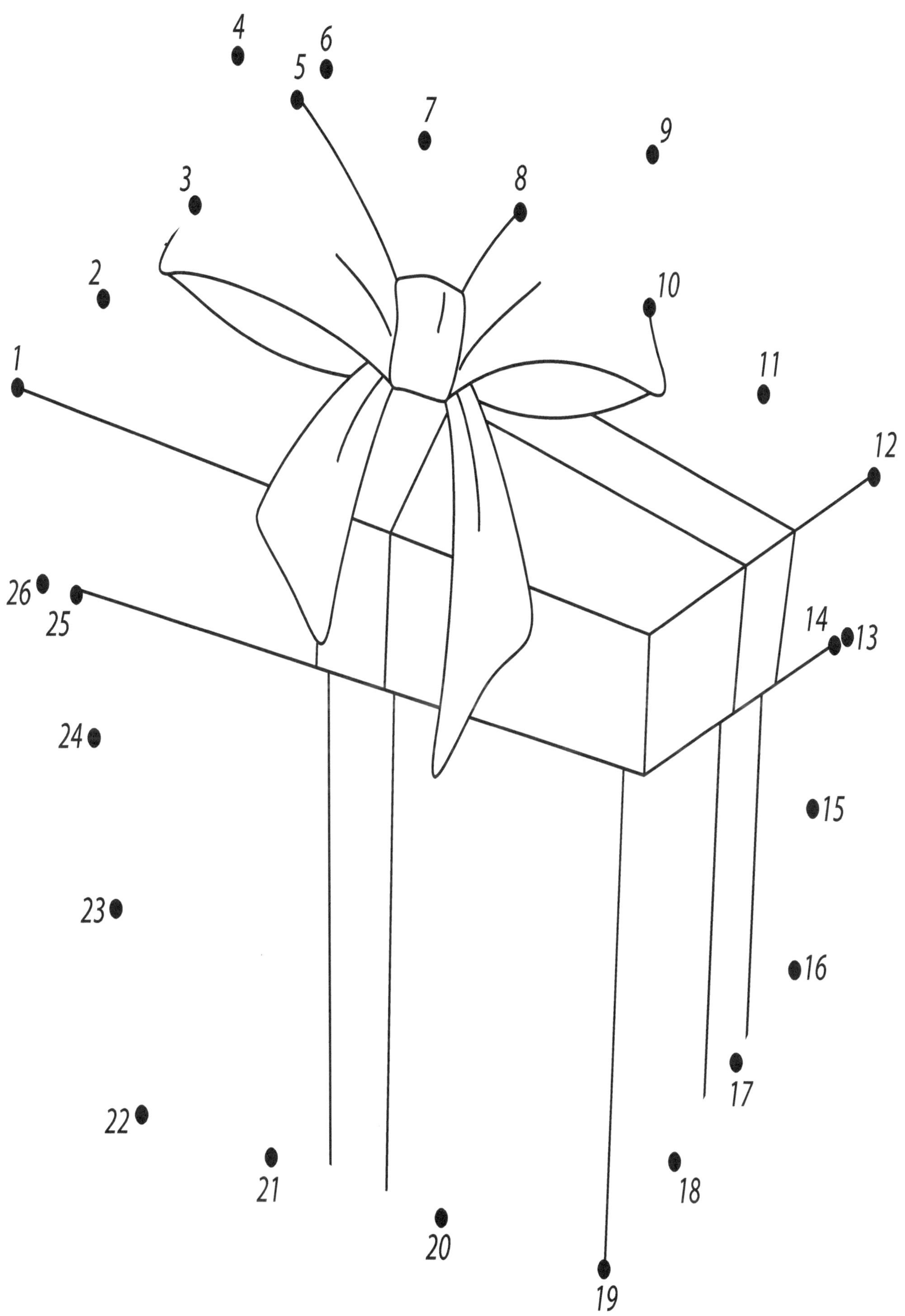

Follow the maze lines from the puppy to the cake. Then color the pictures.

Happy
Birthday

Color, cut, and glue the cupcake on another sheet of paper.

Cut & Glue
COLOR
CUT OUT
GLUE
USE EXAMPLE OR YOUR IMAGINATION
1
2
3

Which maze should the bear follow? Choose the correct maze and then color the pictures.

Start at the X to complete the maze. Then color the cupcake. Do you want cupcakes or cake for your birthday?

____

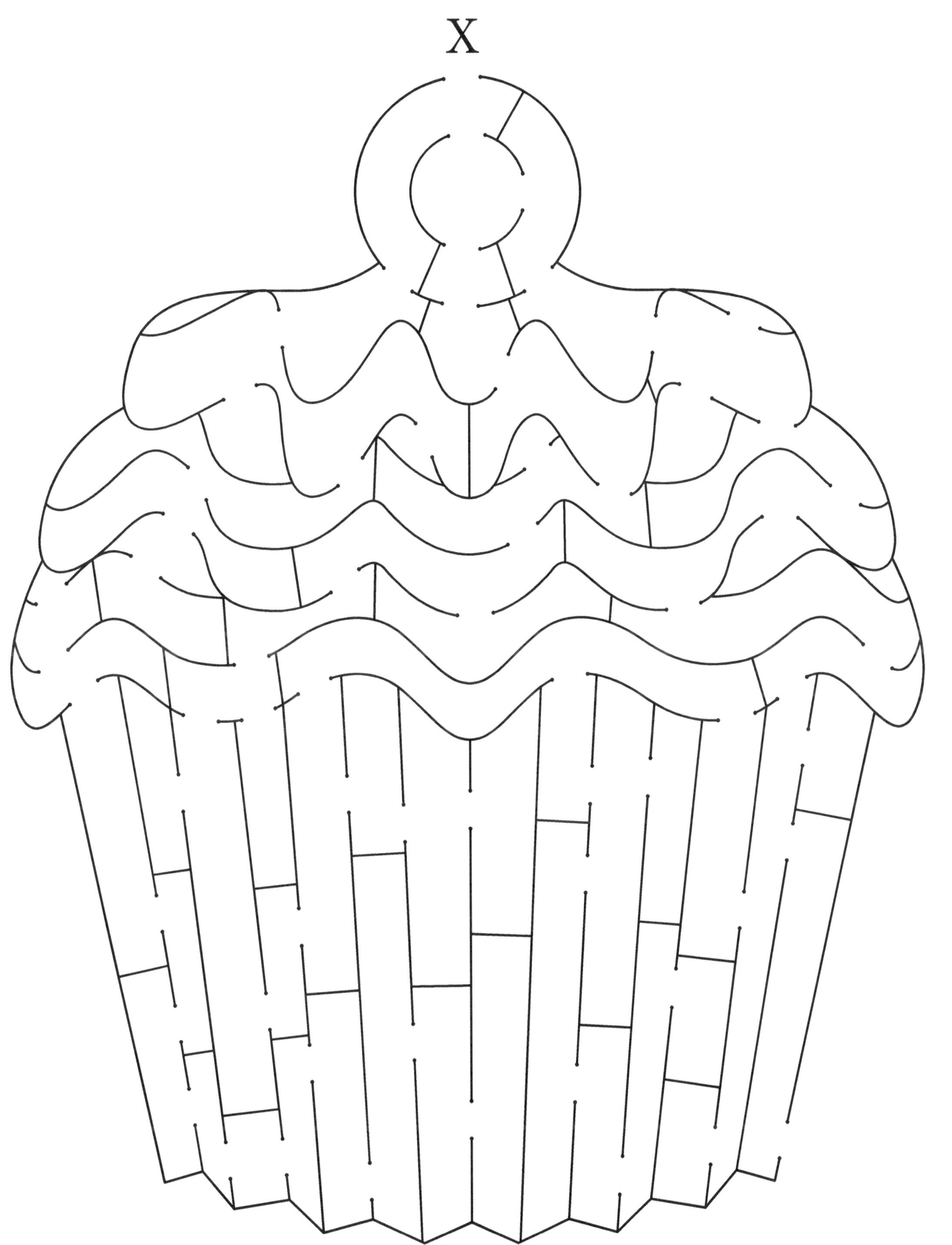
X

Start at the X to help the clown at the top reach the juggling clown at the bottom.

X

Connect the dots and
color the delicious cake!

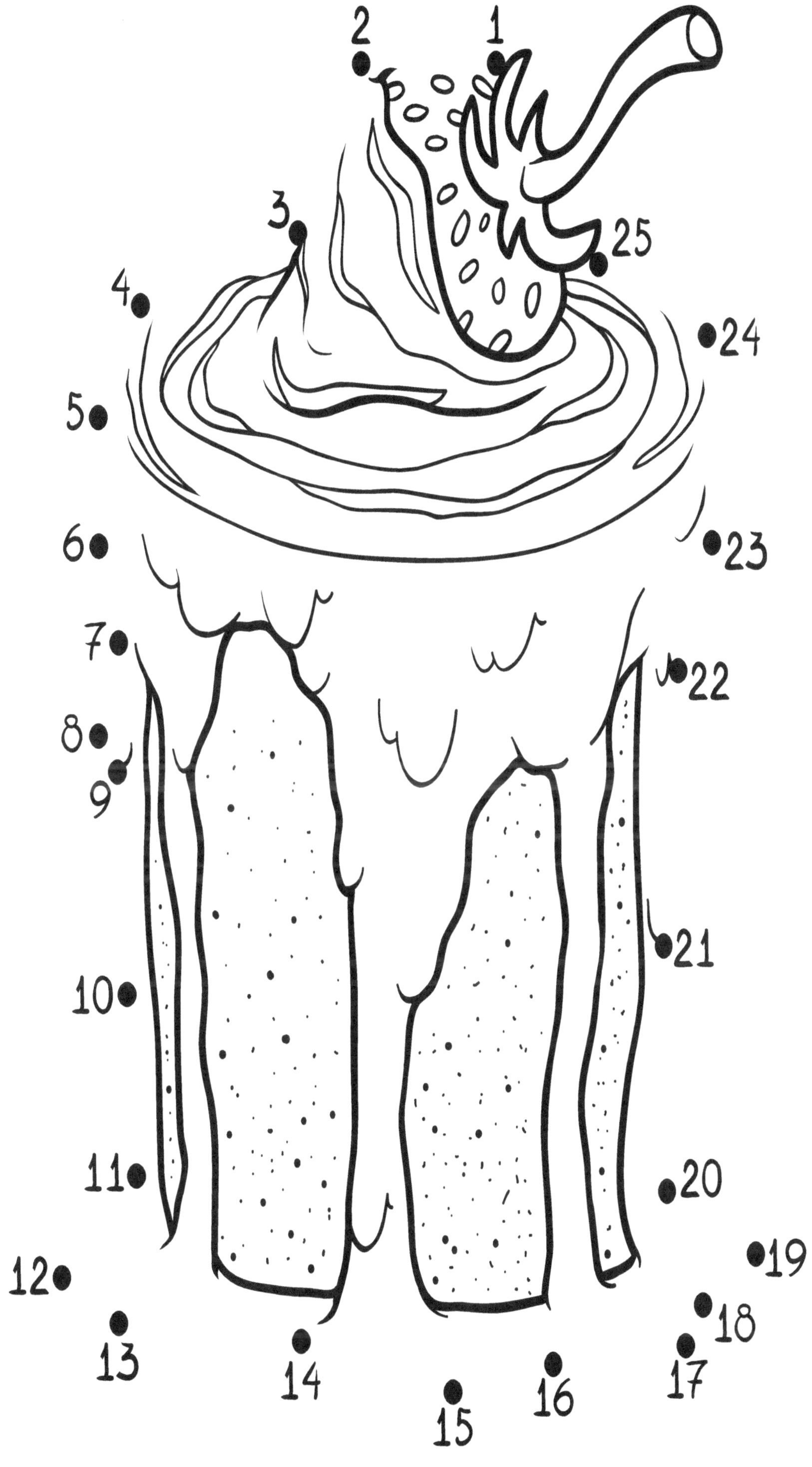

Draw your birthday bow on the grid. Then color the bow with your favorite color(s)! What are your favorite colors?

____

Copy and color the picture of the bow!

Color, cut, and glue your birthday clown on another sheet of paper.

CUT & GLUE
COLOR
1
CUT OUT
2
GLUE
3
USE EXAMPLE OR
YOUR IMAGINATION

Start at the X to complete the maze. Then color your birthday cake! Do you need to add more candles?

BROTHER, don't forget to make a wish
before you blow out your candles!

Color the puppy and your party decorations! The puppy loves birthday gifts, too!

Use the arrows to help the
unicorns reach each other?

Connect the dots and color the bow! How about adding polka dots or stripes to decorate the bow?

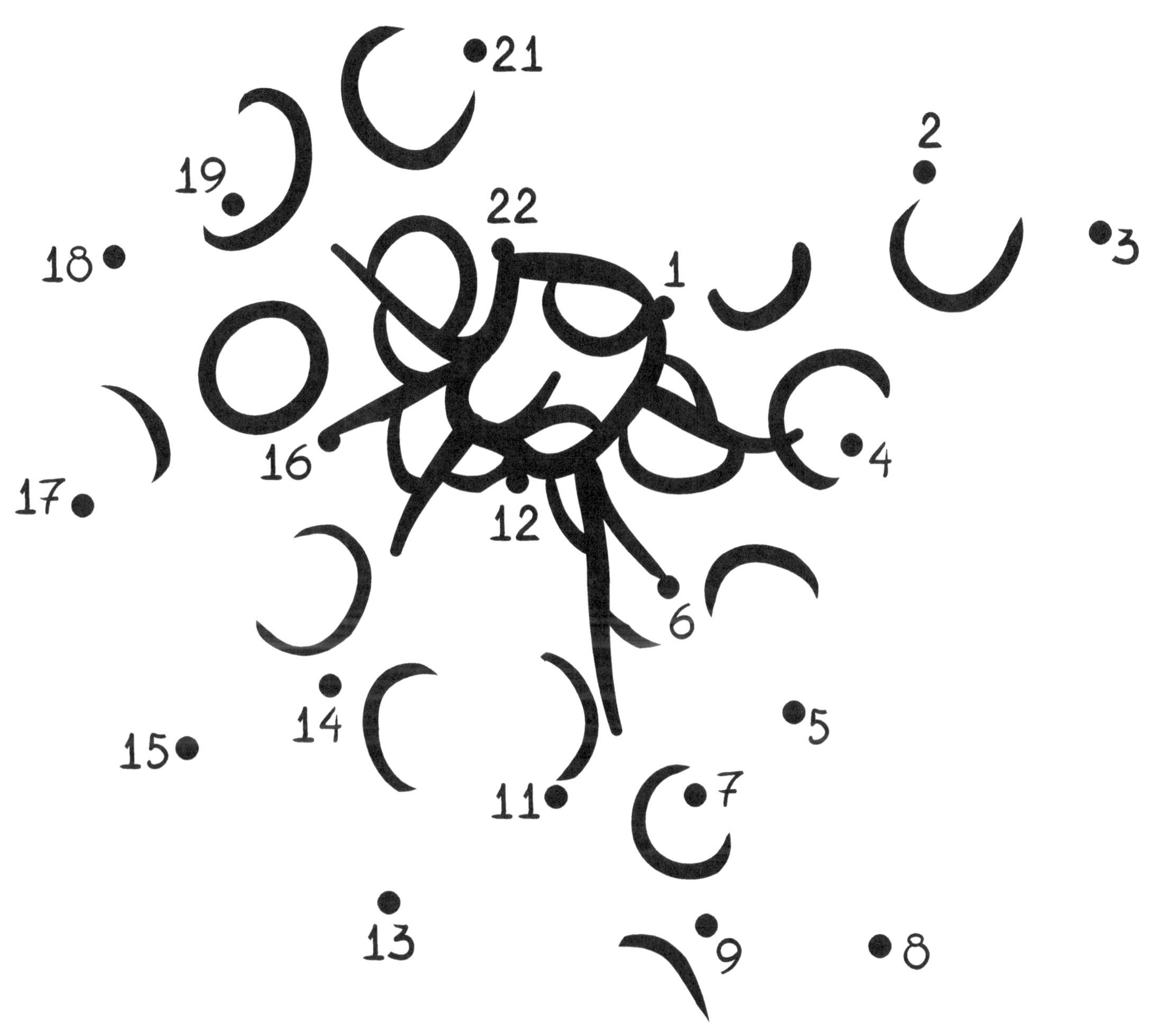

THIS ACTIVITY BOOK
IS A GIFT FOR AN
EXTRAORDINARY
BROTHER!

HAPPY
BIRTHDAY

HAPPY BIRTHDAY BROTHER!
FUN ACTIVITY BOOK:
Mazes, Coloring, Connect the Dots, Counting, & More!
Copyright 2018
By Florabella Publishing, LLC
florabellapublishing@yahoo.com